LANGUAGE ARTS

EXPLORER JUNIOR

How to Write a Report

by Cecilia Minden
and Kate Roth

CHERRY LAKE PUBLISHING · ANN ARBOR, MICHIGAN

CHERRY LAKE
Publishing

Published in the United States of America by Cherry Lake Publishing
Ann Arbor, Michigan
www.cherrylakepublishing.com

Content Adviser: Jeannette Mancilla-Martinez, EdD, Assistant Professor of Literacy, Language, and Culture, University of Illinois at Chicago

Design and Illustration: The Design Lab

Photo Credits: Page 5, ©Olga Kadroff/Shutterstock, Inc.; page 6, ©Jarno Gonzalez Zarraonandia/Shutterstock, Inc.; page 9, ©Dmitriy Shironosov/Dreamstime.com; page 16, ©EpicStockMedia/Shutterstock, Inc.; page 20, ©iStockphoto.com/laflor

Library of Congress Cataloging-in-Publication Data
Minden, Cecilia.
  How to write a report/by Cecilia Minden and Kate Roth.
      p. cm.—(Language arts explorer junior)
  Includes bibliographical references and index.
  ISBN-13: 978-1-61080-105-8 (lib. bdg.)
  ISBN-13: 978-1-61080-278-9 (pbk.)
  1. Language arts (Elementary) 2. English language—Composition and exercises—Study and teaching. 3. Report writing—Juvenile literature. I. Roth, Kate. II. Title.
  LB1576.M534 2011
  372.62'3—dc22   2011000169

Cherry Lake Publishing would like to acknowledge the work of The Partnership for 21st Century Skills. Please visit www.21stcenturyskills.org for more information.

Printed in the United States of America
Corporate Graphics Inc.
July 2011
CLFA09

Table of Contents

CHAPTER ONE

Sharing Information

What would you like to write a report about?

Your teacher has asked you to write a **report**. You must **conduct research** to find more information on the **topic** you will be writing about. Your report will organize and explain your research for others to read. It will tell people what you have learned. A report must do three things to inform the reader about your topic:

1. A report **focuses** on one part of the topic.
2. A report **organizes** information.
3. A report shows the research.

Reports are a good way to share the exciting information you learn from books and other sources.

CHAPTER TWO

Keep It Simple!

A report about Peru might include information about the ruins at Machu Picchu.

A report would be long and boring if it listed everything about a topic! Instead, you should choose a few main points to write about. Let's say your new neighbors are from Peru. You want to learn more about their country. A graphic organizer called a web can help you decide which information to include.

ACTIVITY

Make a Web!

HERE'S WHAT YOU'LL NEED:
- A pencil and paper

INSTRUCTIONS:
1. Choose the topic you will write about in your report.
2. Write the topic in the middle of your paper. Draw a circle around it.
3. Think of six categories that deal with your main topic.
4. Write the categories in the space around the main topic. Circle each subtopic category and draw a line connecting it to the main topic.
5. Highlight at least two categories that you plan to focus on in your report.

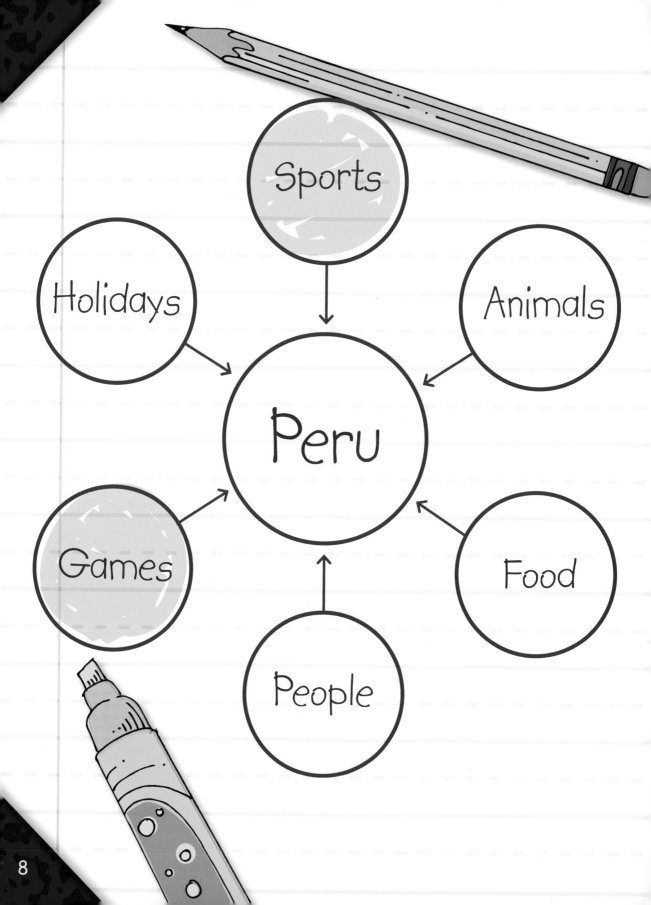

Sports

Holidays

Animals

Peru

Games

Food

People

CHAPTER THREE

Getting Ready to Research

Computers can help you gather and organize information for your report.

The next step is to conduct your research. This is when many writers use a graphic organizer called a KWL chart. *KWL* stands for "what you **k**now," "what you **w**ant to know," and "what you've **l**earned." This chart helps you see where you need to do more research to complete your report.

Create a KWL Chart!

HERE'S WHAT YOU'LL NEED:
- A pencil and paper (or a computer and a printer)

INSTRUCTIONS:
1. Draw a straight line across the top of your paper.
2. Draw two straight lines through your first line all the way to the bottom of the paper. You should now have three columns.
3. Label the first column with a "K," the second with a "W," and the third with an "L."
4. In the first column, write a list of facts you already know about your topic.
5. In the second column, make a list of what you want to learn.
6. The third column is where you will list what you learn. Fill this column in as you conduct your research.

Sample KWL Chart

SPORTS/GAMES IN PERU

K	W	L
What I know	What I want to know	What I've learned
The most popular sports in Peru are soccer and volleyball.	Which other sports do kids play there?	
The climate in Peru varies depending on what part of the country you are in.	What games do kids play outdoors there?	
Lima is the capital of Peru. Lima is by the ocean.	Do kids in Lima play many water sports?	

CHAPTER FOUR

Find the Facts!

Conduct your research by looking at books, magazines, newspapers, and DVDs that discuss your topic. You can also conduct research online. Be careful! Just because information is on the computer does not mean it is true. Have an adult help you decide which Web sites to visit.

Write any important facts and **statistics** you find on note cards. Also mention where you found your information. Make sure you do not simply copy what other people have said. You can either state information a different way or explain that you are **quoting** someone else.

Books and magazines are two places you can find information.

Research Your Topic!

HERE'S WHAT YOU'LL NEED:
- Books, magazines, newspapers, and DVDs
- A pencil
- Note cards

INSTRUCTIONS:
1. Gather your research materials.
2. Write each new fact and statistic you find on a note card.
3. On the bottom of each card, record where you found the information.

Sample Research Note Card

Surfing in Lima, Peru

The weather in Lima is good for surfing because it is usually warm. There is also not much rain.

Peru Surf Guides
www.perusurfguides.com

Next you must decide what information to use from your research. Go back to your KWL chart. Filling in the chart will help you organize your facts and statistics.

Organize Your Information!

HERE'S WHAT YOU'LL NEED:
- Note cards
- Your KWL chart
- A pencil

INSTRUCTIONS:
1. Reread the information you collected on your note cards.
2. Write down each fact or statistic in the "L" column. These will answer the questions in the "W" column.

Sample KWL Chart

SPORTS/GAMES IN PERU

K	W	L
What I know	What I want to Know	What I've learned
The most popular sports in Peru are soccer and volleyball.	Which other sports do Kids play there?	Surfing, sailing, and tennis.
The climate in Peru varies depending on what part of the country you are in.	What games do Kids play outdoors there?	Four Square, played with four players and a Kickball.
Lima is the capital of Peru. Lima is by the ocean.	Do Kids in Lima play many water sports?	They sail and surf. "The waves in Lima are the longest on Earth." (Peru Surf Guides)

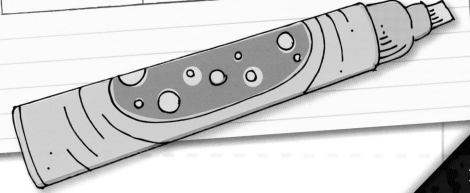

CHAPTER FIVE

The Final Report

It is time to write your report! Begin by writing an opening paragraph that explains the main topic. Get the reader's attention. A question is

Interesting details make it easy for your readers to imagine what it's like to go surfing in Peru.

a good way to begin. You may also share a quote or an interesting statistic.

The **body** of your report comes after the opening. Write a paragraph for each of the categories you researched. Include a **heading** for each topic to let readers know what is coming next. Use your KWL chart to decide which information to include in the body.

Wrap everything up by restating the main idea of your report. At the end of your report, include a picture that supports your topic. A map or **diagram** can be helpful. Now the only thing your report needs is a title. The title should state the topic of your report.

Lima, Peru

Write Your Report!

HERE'S WHAT YOU'LL NEED:
- Your KWL chart
- A pencil and paper (or a computer and a printer)

INSTRUCTIONS:
1. Write an opening paragraph.
2. Write a paragraph for each category in the body of your report. Remember to include headings!
3. Write an ending statement.
4. Give your report a title.

Sports and Games in Peru

Can you imagine living in a city where it almost never rains? The weather in Lima, Peru, is usually sunny and warm. Soccer is a favorite sport to play outside. Volleyball is popular on the sandy beaches. I wondered what other sports kids in Peru like to play outside. I learned that surfing is also popular.

Surfing

The western side of Peru is on the Pacific Ocean. Surfing is a fun way to spend the day on the coast. Surfers stand on a long, narrow board and ride a wave into the shore. People in Peru say their country's waves are "the longest on Earth." I found this information on a Web site called Peru Surf Guides.

Four Square

Four Square is for kids who would rather play on dry land. A big square is drawn or painted on a flat surface outside. Then lines are drawn to divide the big square into four smaller squares. Four players each take a corner. One player kicks the ball into another player's square. The object is to keep the ball out of your square. The ball can only bounce one time. You have to be quick!

Kids all over the world play sports to have fun. If you lived in Peru, what sport would you choose? Soccer, volleyball, surfing , or Four Square?

CHAPTER SIX

Reread Your Writing!

Don't forget to check your report for any grammar or spelling mistakes. Will you read your report to your class or hang it somewhere in the classroom? Everyone will enjoy finding out all that you have learned!

Double check your work to make sure it is just the way you want it.

STOP!
DON'T WRITE
IN THE BOOK!

ACTIVITY

Do a Final Check!

Ask yourself these questions as you reread your report:

☐ YES ☐ NO   Do I report on one main topic?

☐ YES ☐ NO   Do I mention at least two categories that deal with my topic?

☐ YES ☐ NO   Do I use my research to explain what I learned?

☐ YES ☐ NO   Do I include a title in my report?

☐ YES ☐ NO   Do I organize my information into an opening, a body, and a closing?

☐ YES ☐ NO   Do I have a heading for each of the paragraphs in the body?

☐ YES ☐ NO   Do I use correct grammar and spelling?

Glossary

body (BAH-dee) the main part of a report

category (KAT-ih-gor-ee) an idea within a main topic

conduct (kuhn-DUHKT) carry out

graphic organizer (GRA-fik OR-guh-ni-zur) a drawing that helps organize ideas

heading (HE-ding) the title of a paragraph

quoting (KWOT-ing) repeating someone's exact words

report (ri-PORT) a writing project that shares information about a certain topic

research (REE-surch) the act of collecting information about a topic

statistics (steh-TIS-tiks) a collection of numbers that deal with a certain topic

topic (TAH-pik) subject

For More Information

BOOKS

Bentley, Nancy. *Don't Be a Copycat! Write a Great Report Without Plagiarizing.* Berkeley Heights, NJ: Enslow Publishers, 2008.

Herman, Gail. *Make-a-Splash Writing Rules.* Pleasantville, NY: Gareth Stevens Publishers, 2010.

WEB SITES

Kids.gov—Social Studies
www.kids.gov/k_5/k_5_social.shtml
Check out this site for topics for social studies reports.

Scholastic: Write a Winning Research Report
www.scholastic.com/resources/article/write-a-winning-research-report
Discover more tips for writing great research reports.

Index

About the Authors

Cecilia Minden, PhD, is the former director of the Language and Literacy Program at Harvard Graduate School of Education. She earned her doctorate from the University of Virginia. While at Harvard, Dr. Minden also taught several writing courses. Her research focuses on early literacy skills and developing phonics curriculums. She is now a full-time literacy consultant and the author of more than 100 books for children. Dr. Minden lives with her family in Chapel Hill, North Carolina. She likes to write early in the morning while the house is still quiet.

Kate Roth has a doctorate from Harvard University in language and literacy and a master's degree from Columbia University Teachers College in curriculum and teaching. Her work focuses on writing instruction in the primary grades. She has taught kindergarten, first grade, and Reading Recovery. She has also instructed hundreds of teachers around the world in early-literacy practices. She lives in Shanghai, China, with her husband and three children, ages 2, 6, and 9. Together they do a lot of writing to stay in touch with friends and family and to record their experiences.